MW01537843

THIS JOURNAL BELONGS TO:

Made in the USA
Las Vegas, NV
03 August 2024

93312286R00069